Introduction

και ο λογος σαρξ εγενετο – kai ho Logos sarx ginomai – and the Word was made flesh (John 1:14)

The word 'made' was translated from the Greek word 'ginomai' . The same base word 'ginomai' is used in Hebrews 4:3 when it says God *finished or completed* His work. God has spoken such a complete and final word in Christ Jesus, that throughout the ages to come He will continue to unfold the exceeding greatness of His kindness toward us, that happened in this event, without ever exhausting the subject. (Eph 2:7)

There has been a growing need for a course that presents the success of what Jesus has done, with uncompromising clarity. So many have asked: "...we want to immerse ourselves in this message; we also want a way of introducing others to a solid foundation in this revelation of God's favour." And so this course was born.

In Collosians 2:2 Paul speaks about the riches or wealth that comes from being fully persuaded ... a persuasion that comes through understanding. These courses are designed for this very purpose ... not to confuse students with many opinions ... but to boldly expound the meaning of Christ Jesus, in the full assurance that God has made His mind known in Christ. (1 Cor 2:16)

How it works

The same Word that became flesh in Christ, desires to become flesh in you ... to find tangible expression through your life.

The ultimate destiny of the Word, was never a book, but the image and likeness of God displayed in human life!

This study guide to the written Word, is designed for this very purpose: to inspire and ignite an understanding that will find expression through our lives – the Word made flesh. The course is therefore not designed to overload students with information, but rather to teach each one how to draw out, the implanted word.

Both the content and the method in which the course is presented is aimed at this purpose. The course consists of 25 weekly modules. Each module has the following components:

The Lesson.
Each lesson is concise - short and clear. Additional references are provided in the footnotes of each lesson, if further study is desired. The benefit of this approach is that you can spend as little as 10 minutes, or as much time as

you would like to on each lesson.

Meditation.

The main lesson is followed by a 'Meditation' scripture. The first module in this course is all about meditation, and will help you to draw the maximum value out of each lesson. In a nutshell, meditation is a way of stirring up, drawing out and reminding yourself of this scripture daily. Maybe learn it off by heart, and take the time to simply be still and let it speak to you.

Affirmation.

The meditation section is followed by 'Affirmation'. I would encourage you to speak this out loud. The affirmation is basically a conclusion ... or an implication of the lesson.

Discussion.

Ideally a small group of people will work through the material together. The 'Discussion' section offers a few questions to help groups focus their discussion. Ultimately, the Word made flesh, means that it will ignite a life-long conversation!

Assignment.

Writing down our thoughts, is of greatest benefit to ourselves even though it could benefit others as well. Developing a habit of writing will soon transform this activity into the most exciting part of the course.

Many studies have shown how the practise of writing one's thoughts, is of greater benefit than simply discussing them!

Consider joining the online course which offers live discussions and constructive comments on the assignments.

WEEK 1
MEDITATION

I will remember my song in the night; I will meditate with my heart, And my spirit ponders:
I will meditate on all Your work And muse on Your deeds.
Ps 77:6,12

Finally, brothers, whatever is true, whatever is honorable, whatever is just, whatever is pure, whatever is lovely, whatever is commendable, if there is any excellence, if there is anything worthy of praise, think about these things.
Phil 4:8

Many concepts and images can be conjured up by the word 'meditation'. However the practice of meditation, as taught in the scriptures, is both simple and powerful.

In many belief systems the practice of meditation is aimed at clearing the mind of everything. However, meditation as described in the scriptures has a very definite focus.

There are many things competing for our attention, but only some are worthy of our attention. Jesus taught that worry, anxiety, the cares of this world, can choke the life we were designed for. His advice is clear: rather focus on how your Father values you!

"If God gives such attention to the appearance of wildflowers—most of which are never even seen—don't you think he'll attend to you, take pride in you, do his best for you? What I'm trying to do here is to get you to relax, to not be so preoccupied with getting, so you can respond to God's giving. People who don't know God and the way he works fuss over these things, but you know both God and how he works. Steep your life in God-reality, God-initiative, God-provisions."
Mt 6:30-33 MSG

So, part of meditation is deliberately excluding some thoughts … thoughts that distract you from God's thoughts about you.[1] Practically this can be done by deliberately setting your mind on other things. Instead of worrying about food, look at the birds and consider how your Father feeds them. Instead of worrying about your clothing, look at the flowers of the fields and consider how your Father clothes them.

Meditation is not limited to silent thoughts. The idea of speaking to yourself … muttering, is very much part of it.[2] Obviously it would be good if one can find a peaceful environment in which to meditate, but most people have busy days and little spare time. Meditation need not be limited to quiet times when you are on your own. In the

1 1 Cor 2:2
2 Col 3:16, Eph 5:19

midst of any activity, you can mutter the scriptures to yourself; you can find opportunity to remind yourself of His thoughts towards you.

Paul instructed that we pray continually, without ceasing.[3] This kind of prayer is so much more than a ritualistic event, it is an uninterrupted awareness of His presence.

To make time to be on your own, to give your entire attention to Him will always be precious, but never limit your awareness of Him to such moments.

There is a vast difference between pushing information into someone, and pulling knowledge out of someone! You might be surprised that the attitude of all the new testament writers was not to inform their audience, but to teach them how to access and draw out the implanted word, the inherent knowledge.

Paul once wrote that all the treasures of wisdom and knowledge are hidden in Christ[4] ... and Christ is in you! Another time he writes that we have been enriched in everything - in all knowledge and the ability to express it.[5]

---

3 1 Thes 5:17
4 Col 2:3
5 1 Cor 1:5

John wrote this amazing statement: "*you know all things. I have not written to you because you do not know the truth, but because you know it*".[6] His purpose in writing was not because he knew something they didn't know, but it was to stir up the knowledge within them.

Peter said it this way: "*For this reason I will not be negligent to remind you always of these things, though you know and are established in the present truth. Yes, I think it is right, as long as I am in this tent, to stir you up by reminding you*" 2 Pet 1:12,13

Can you perceive what they understood? There is a wealth of untapped understanding in man. We are called to stir it up, to remind ourselves and mankind of what we inherently know.

Each week has one scripture for meditation. The wealth and depth hidden in those words are inexhaustible. It won't be hard to learn it off by heart and thereby have it ready, at any time, to bring it to mind and allow His Spirit to enlighten you about its meaning.

---

6 1 John 2:20,21

Meditation:

Instead, his delight is in the LORD's instruction,
and he meditates on it day and night.
He is like a tree planted beside streams of water
that bears its fruit in season
and whose leaf does not wither.
Whatever he does prospers.
Psalms 1:2,3 Holmans

Affirmation:

I delight in the Word of my Lord. He captivates my thoughts day and night. From His limitless resources I continually draw sustenance.

Discussion:

- Discuss the practice of meditation and Paul's statement: "you have been enriched in everything - in all knowledge and the ability to express it"
- How can you make meditation part of your daily life?

Assignment:

Write a short essay about 1 John 2:20,21. Show how you already have a limitless source of revelation and knowledge within you, and explore the ways in which this can be drawn out.

Week 2
Understanding the Bible

(by Francois du Toit)

The Bible is a dangerous book! It has confused and divided more people than any other document. Yet its profound and simple message continues to appeal, overwhelm and transform the lives of multitudes of men and women of any age or culture. It is still the best seller on the planet.

If it is such a dangerous document, how does one approach the book? What is the key that unlocks its mystery message?

The romance of the ages is revealed here. The heart of the Lover, our Maker is hidden in scripture and uncovered in the pages of this book. He says in Isa 65:1 "*I was ready to be found by those who did not seek me. I said, Here am I, here am I.*"

What would it be that attracts God to engage with man?
Man began in God!
Man is the greatest idea that God had ever had!
It is not our brief history on planet earth that introduces us to God. He has always known us. God knew you before he formed you in your mother's womb![1]

1 Jer 1:5

The Bible records how the invisible engineer of the universe found expression of his image and likeness in visible form in human life! When God imagined you, he thought of you on equal terms as he would of himself; a being whose intimate friendship would intrigue him for eternity. Man would be partner in God's triune oneness!

Jesus says in John 10:30 "*I and the Father are one.*" And again in John 14:20, "*In that day you will know that I am in my Father, and you in me, and I in you.*" God has found us in Christ before he lost us in Adam! He associated us in Christ before the foundation of the world.[2] He has always known us; now in Christ he invites us to know ourselves even as we have always been known![3]

Jesus Christ is the context and meaning of scripture; his work of redeeming the image and likeness of God in man, is what the Bible is all about![4] . The whole Bible is about Jesus and Jesus is all about you! This makes the Bible the most relevant book.

Initially the prophetic shadow of the Old Testament introduces us to the Promise. He is the Messiah-Christ, the Incarnate Word. He represents the entire human race.

---

2 Eph 1:4
3 1 Cor 13:12
4 Col.1:13-15

In the economy of God, Jesus mirrors humanity. The heart dream of God realized in the redemption of man; in one man, through one act of righteousness, in a single sacrifice! Rom 5:18 The conclusion is clear: it took just one offence to condemn mankind; one act of righteousness declares the same mankind innocent.

When Jesus joins the two confused disciples on their way back from Jerusalem he introduces himself to them through the eyes of scripture: Luk 24:27 "*And beginning with Moses and all the prophets, he interpreted to them in all the scriptures the things concerning himself.*" Also in Luk 24:44,45 he does the same when he appears to his disciples: "*He said to them, "These are my words which I spoke to you, while I was still with you, that everything written about me in the law of Moses and the prophets and the psalms must be fulfilled. Then he opened their minds to understand the scriptures.*"

The destiny of the Logos was not intended to be caged in a book or a doctrine but to be documented and unveiled in human life! Human life is the most articulate voice of scripture. Jesus is God's language; mankind is his audience. Heb 1:1-3

Diligent research and study is not the key to understanding the scriptures; Jesus says, "*You study and search the scriptures thinking that in them you will find eternal life, but if you miss me, you miss the point.*" The Message translation reads, "*You have your heads in your Bibles constantly because you think you'll find eternal life there. But you miss the forest for the trees. These Scriptures are all about me!*" John 5:39. Jesus is the context of scripture. Isa.53:4,5.

Long before the first line of scripture
was penned on papyrus scroll,
the Word, unwritten,
existed as the mind of God.

Before the books were gathered
collated as sacred text,
the Word, intangible; invisible,
was planning, was ordering
the ages that were to come.

This Word predates the Bible,
this Word predates creation,
this Word is alive and active
and speaking still today.
(Andre Rabe)

24

MEDITATION:

You have your heads in your Bibles constantly because you think you'll find eternal life there. But you miss the forest for the trees. These Scriptures are all about me!
John 5:39 MSG

AFFIRMATION:

The Scriptures point to a reality greater than themselves: Christ in me!

Discussion:

- Discuss the Word that was in the beginning, before the scriptures.
- What is the value of scripture?
- What do the scriptures point to?

Assignment:

Write a short essay about the destiny of the word. In that context also describe the value of the scriptures and the key to understanding them.

Week 3
Who is God?

Before creation, before time and space, God is.
Long before science confirmed that the universe had a beginning and that time is related to space, the scriptures spoke of a dimension beyond time and space.[1] He is the only Creator through whom everything was made and by whom it is kept in existence.[2] There are depths and mysteries in God beyond anything we are familiar with in this created realm. These mysteries would have remained veiled forever if He did not take the initiative to reveal Himself. The God who is beyond our wildest imaginations, has revealed Himself in the person of Christ Jesus.[3]

God is One … yet more than one!
One in that there is no confusion, no contradiction, no competing or opposing qualities in Him.[4]
'More than one' in that He is love and love by its very nature does not exist in isolation or singularity, but in relationship.[5] This relationship in God is often described in terms of Father, Son and Spirit. God in essence, is a relationship of love.[6]

---

1 2 Tim 1:9
2 John 1:1-5, 1 Cor 8:6
3 John 1:18, 1 Cor 2:16, 1 John 5:20
4 1 Cor 14:33, 1 John 1:5, James 1:17
5 1 John 4:8,9
6 John 14:16,17

Understanding this … that God is love … gives us insight into the motivation behind all of creation. God was not bored, lonely or needy. It was the overflow of love, the vibrant, dynamic exchange between those in this God-union that gave birth to the idea of man.[7] His dream was nothing less than the expansion of this intimacy … an expansion that would not diminish the quality.[8] For such a quality of love to be expanded, the being He imagined would be nothing less than their image and likeness.[9] Father & Son incorporated, would become Father & Sons incorporated.[10]

Nowhere is the character of God more accurately revealed than in the person of Christ Jesus.[11] We'll look at that in more detail in later studies.

---

7 Eph 1:4
8 John 17:21-24
9 Gen 1:26
10 Rom 8:29
11 Heb 1:1-3

28

MEDITATION:

Yet for us there is [only] one God, the Father, Who is the Source of all things and for Whom we [have life], and one Lord, Jesus Christ, through and by Whom are all things and through and by Whom we [ourselves exist].
1 Cor 8:6 AMP

AFFIRMATION:

God is the source of all things. He imagined me, created me and sustains me in existence.

Discussion:

- What motivated God to create?
- Why is His motivation important?
- How do we understand this realm before time and space?

Assignment:

Write a short essay about the activity of God before creation. Use some scriptural references to show what occupied Him before time began.

Week 4
Light, Life, Love

Light

John describes God as light, life, and love.

God is light and in Him is no darkness at all. His light is not just any light, it is absolute light. Darkness cannot understand or overcome it. Light is not a passive quality - it's dynamic, explosive. Light desires to shine! This is God; He desires to reveal Himself. He is not withdrawn, un-knowable and hidden. He is light, and He desires to enlighten every man with the knowledge of His favour. While Paul was hunting down the followers of Jesus Christ, Jesus revealed Himself to Paul. Later Paul writes about the God who reveals Himself to those who do not seek Him! He makes His sun to shine on the evil and the good. It is in His nature to reveal Himself; it has nothing to do with your ability to attain revelation, it has everything to do with His desire to reveal Himself, independent of you deserving or not deserving it!

John 1:4: "*In him was life; and the life was the light of men.*"

John 1:9: "*He was the true Light which enlightens every person coming into the world.*"

The life Jesus lived, is the light of man. His life reveals who mankind really is. Jesus was not just an example for man, but of man! Light allows us to appreciate the beauty and value of something. Darkness covers and hides things to such an extent that we are not even certain of its existence - but when light comes, we suddenly see the reality of what darkness denied. Light persuades us firstly of the existence of the object and then reveals its beauty.

Life

God is life, and in Him is no death at all! The Greek word for this God-kind of life is 'Zoe'. It has the meaning of absolute life in it. Jesus spoke about this life as abundant life.[1] At another time He described it as a spring of living water bursting forth from within you.[2] Again, this is no passive quality. God is not passive; He brims over with life. He lives abundantly, and desires to share this abundant life. His life is so expansive and so full of goodness that He simply has to share it.

When the life within a fruit tree becomes more than what it needs to sustain itself, it produces fruit. This fruit contains the seed for another tree. This abundance of life within the tree spills over and reproduced itself. It is the abundance of life in God, that spilled over and produced man. The

1 John 10:10
2 John 4:13

glorious life He enjoyed was more than He needed for Himself. The desire to share this extravagance, resulted in creation.

Love

God is love. Love's greatest need is to give. This is no passive love either, but a love that manifests itself. He demonstrated His love toward us, in that while we were at enmity against Him, He reconciled us to Himself![3] While the world was still spitting in His face and breathing out hatred against Him, He kissed the world and declared that their trespasses would no longer be held against them.[4] This is a love so great that it could not wait for man to approach, but took the initiative to embrace us while we were still hostile.

God's Expressive Nature.

We so often limit our perceptions to our own points of view. We see the love of God only within the context of our own need. But it is not so much our need for His love that caused Him to reach out to us, as it is His own desire to simply love. It is not just the intensity of the darkness we are in, that motivates Him to bring light. It is simply His nature to shine forth.

God delights in revealing Himself. He overflows with life. He brims over with love. He bursts forth with light. At the

3 Rom 5:10, Eph 2:16
4 2 Cor 5:19

very core of who God is, is this urgency to express Himself; to manifest Himself; to demonstrate His love. The whole of the universe is testimony to His enormous desire and ability to express Himself. Every galaxy, every plant, every animal is a unique manifestation of His imagination. But ultimately a person wants to express Himself through a personality and that's why God made you!

MEDITATION:

He was the true Light which enlightens every person coming into the world.
John 1:9

AFFIRMATION:

He enlightens me! I am who God reveals me to be. I am not defined by anything else, but God's opinion of me.

Discussion:

- What does 'God is light' mean to you?
- What is 'Love's' greatest desire?
- Discuss Jesus' definition of eternal life (John 17:3)

Assignment:

Write a short essay about the expressive nature of God, linking that to His expression in and through you.

Week 5
Who is Man?

The most authentic definition of man was given by our designer Himself.

Genesis begins with an account of creation. When God created, He would speak to the substance from which He wanted to make something new and tell it to bring forth. So He says to the earth: "...earth, bring forth grass and herbs and tress … and the earth brought forth grass …"[1]

In the same way, when He created man, there was a part that was made from the earth, but there was also another part... God again speaks to the substance from which He wants to make man and says: "Us, bring forth man ...our image and our likeness"![2] There is a part of man that has its origin, its substance, in God Himself!

Why did God invest so much in man? Remember who God is - He is a relationship of love. He will settle for nothing less than the same quality of intimacy that exists within Himself.[3] That means that man had to be a God-kind of being; a being that could appreciate, receive and respond with the same quality of love that is within God. God designed man to be God-compatible, able to participate

1 Gen 1:11,12
2 Gen 1:26
3 1 Cor 1:9

in this circle of love.[4]

God has never given up on His idea to see His image and likeness displayed in human life. This blueprint of man's design - the perfect man[5] - was preserved in Christ Jesus to be revealed at the right time. In Christ Jesus, He came to redeem and restore what He always saw in man.

---

4 2 Pet 1:4
5 Eph 4:13

38

Meditation:

Then God said, "Let Us make man in Our image, according to Our likeness"
Gen 1:26 NKJV

Affirmation:

I am the image and likeness of God!

Discussion:

- What does it mean to be made in the image and likeness of God?.
- What is the significance of your origin?

Assignment:

Write a short essay about the essence of man based on what we learn from the creation of man.

Week 6
What went wrong?

In short, Adam and Eve never realised the depth of relationship God designed them for. They never recognised the image and likeness to the extent they were capable of.

The story of the temptation and fall of man is recorded in Genesis 3.

There is so much to be learned from it:

The temptation was an external voice - man was not flawed by design or evil from within.

The tempter thrived on man's ignorance, evident in the suggestion that " *...if you eat this fruit ... you will be like God ...*"

The fact was that they were already like God, created in His image and likeness ... ignorance made the temptation appealing.

The tempter also painted a false picture of God suggesting that He did not want man to be like Him!

However, despite all the things man was ignorant of, there was one thing they knew for sure: God said: "*of the tree of the knowledge of good and evil you shall not eat, for in the day that you eat of it you shall surely die.*"[1]

Misunderstanding God and not knowing themselves, was

1 Gen 2:17

the basis of disobeying Him, and choosing an alternative life. Yet this disobedience was not accidental or without guilt, it was a conscious, wilful decision to disobey.

Man, like God, was designed to live in relationship. Innocence is a key ingredient to this relationship. In choosing a lie, in disobeying God, man separated himself from his life-source - God. God still sustained man in existence, but the spontaneous, innocent and vibrant relationship was no longer possible.

Condition of fallen man.

What did this do to man? How did sin and evil affect man? There are some things which changed immediately, other things which changed over a period of time, and yet other things which stayed the same.

What changed immediately?

The scriptures call the disobedience of Adam, sin.[2] Sin was not only an external act, it was an event in which Adam opened himself up to a foreign influence. Immediately, there was another dominion and influence at work in Adam and Eve.

Sin also changed the condition of man from innocent to guilty[3]. Before the fall, man was capable of the highest form

---

2 Rom 5:12

3 Rom 3:23

of intimacy with God. That was no longer possible. A type of relationship was still possible, but not the fullness of what God foresaw.

This act also opened the door for corruption to spread to all men and all creation. The universal effect of this event is described in Rom 5 as follows: "*through one man sin entered the world, and death through sin*"[4]. And because man had dominion over all creation, his condition effected all of creation … it became subject to corruption.[5]

What changed over time?

The foreign influence that man opened himself up to, is a corrupting and ultimately deadly influence.[6] It is a disease that spreads. Man did not immediately become utterly corrupt, perverted and completely separate from God. No. We see God continues in conversation with man even after the fall. We see the God-given qualities of love and relationship continue. But there is a progressive decay and perversion that gets worse and worse.

The purpose of evil is to appose all that is of God. But because evil is not a creative force like God, it can only twist, pervert and suppress what God has made. This is why man is capable of evil beyond any animal. These very

4 Rom 5:12
5 Rom 8:20
6 Rom 7:5

powerful qualities God gave man, were pointed in the opposite direction.

Hope, that joyful expectation for something good, was perverted to become despair - a depressing lack of any good expectation. Faith, the unwavering confidence and reliance in the One who only means to do us good, was twisted to become an irrational fear of imminent destruction and pain. We can go on and on … the point is, every evil quality ever displayed in man, was a perversion of an original good quality.

If evil had its way it would completely destroy man and creation … draw it into the nothingness from which it came. But it has no such power, it has to progressively pull man deeper and deeper into its abyss of decay.

Paul does not mince his words when he describes this condition as 'men who suppress the truth in unrighteousness', 'were not thankful, but became futile in their thoughts, and their foolish hearts were darkened'.[7] Those who show no resistance to evil are described as follows: "*as they did not like to retain God in their knowledge, God gave them over to a debased mind, to do those things which are not fitting; being filled with all unrighteousness, sexual immorality, wickedness, covetousness, maliciousness; full of envy, murder, strife, deceit, evil-mindedness; they are whisperers, backbiters,*

7 Rom 1:18-21

haters of God, violent, proud, boasters, inventors of evil things, disobedient to parents, undiscerning, untrustworthy, unloving, unforgiving, unmerciful"[8]

What did not change?

In Gen 9:6 and numerous other references, God confirms that man is still His image and likeness. The image and likeness that man was created in, is immutable - it cannot be destroyed. Darkness might have dimmed it, the father of lies might have obscured it, wickedness might have twisted man out of his true pattern, but the essence of man has never been completely destroyed.

In Luke 15 Jesus tells us of the lost sheep, the lost coin, the lost son.

The sheep remained a sheep although lost; the coin retained its value, although lost; the son remained a son, although lost. In all three cases the owner remained the owner and committed to that which was lost. The sheep and the coin contributed nothing towards being found. In the case of the son, his situation changed 'when he came to himself' (verse 17)

Even the word lost has the most beautiful promise in it, for you cannot be lost unless you belong!

God still saw enough value in us, to pursue us and save us

8 Rom 1:28-31

at the greatest cost. Mankind was not corrupted beyond the possibility of restoration. Mankind was not lost beyond the possibility of salvation.

Out of all proportion

Although it is important to understand the fall and its consequences, we should always see it in the context of the much greater work of salvation that happened in Christ Jesus.

Religion focuses on the fall of man to the extent that it even defines man by this event. However, we'll see in a later chapter how Christ's work of restoration is out of all proportion to the fall of man.

MEDITATION:

Therefore, just as through one man sin entered the world, and death through sin, and thus death spread to all men, because all sinned.

Therefore, as through one man's offense judgment came to all men, resulting in condemnation, even so through one Man's righteous act the free gift came to all men, resulting in justification of life.
Rom 5:11,18 NKJV

AFFIRMATION:

As surely as I was included in Adam, I am included in Christ Jesus.

Discussion:

- What makes temptation attractive?.
- What makes temptation unattractive?
- What is it in man, even after the fall, that made man so valuable to God?

Assignment:

Write a short essay explaining what God saw in man, even after the fall, that caused Him to pursue us in order to save us.

Week 7
The Law System

Marriage is meant for intimacy and enjoyment - suspicion and distance undermine the very purpose of marriage. One can never replace the spontaneity and freedom of being in love with formality and obligation and still maintain the same quality of relationship.

Lets imagine a scenario in which a husband and wife have had a fight, and seeing that it's just a fantasy, lets say its all the wife's fault! The husband tries to converse, but the situation is so tender that the wife can't face any further confrontation. Silence and distance become her only escape.

Through the days and weeks that follow the situation only gets worse and this results in a separation. The husband observes his wife sinking into a pit of depression but she is not willing to face him or converse with him. However the husband still loves his wife and believes that the relationship can be restored[1], so he makes a practical interim arrangement. In order to prevent her from falling into absolute destitution and despair, he commits to support her and provide for her if she keeps to some basic and

1 Is 49:15,16

reasonable obligations. For instance: remain faithful to him, no other lovers allowed! Very reasonable. A few other tasks are agreed like looking after the house he provides etc.

The only thing these arrangements are supposed to reveal, is that the husband still believes that the relationship can be saved. These arrangements were never meant to replace the original intimate relationship. They were only put in place for her protection and provision until the original relationship is restored. By no means can this situation compete or compare with the spontaneous, intimate relationship they once enjoyed.

Something terrible happens in this arrangement: It gives validity to the distance! The very distance that needs to be destroyed, finds an opportunity within this temporary arrangement to make itself legitimate. This new law-system gives validity to the distance!

And the wife, instead of trying to find a fundamental solution to the problem, now hides behind the fact that she is keeping the rules and therefore deserves the provision. She actually finds this new system very convenient, because she does not have to deal with her husband directly. She feels justified in keeping the rules, and even when she breaks the rules there are ways of correcting the situation without direct contact with him. Her heart grows even harder!

The Law is temporal

The law was never meant to solve the relationship between man and God - it was only an interim arrangement.[2] In a way it revealed something of the heart of God - He still believed the relationship could be restored. But the law was not the way in which He would restore the relationship - it was only given in the context of mankind falling into total destitution and chaos, as an interim way of protecting and providing for man. In Christ the Law is both fulfilled and removed[3], as He restored the intimacy and freedom of the original relationship.

The Law does not solve the problem.

The law never dealt with sin, never brought sin to a final judgement.[4] In fact the problem was intensified within this context. Sin - which was the very distance and separation that resulted from this broken relationship - found an opportunity within the law system. Distance gained a form of validity in the Law! And man, instead of gratefully accepting the provision, uses the law to develop self-righteousness. The Law served to harden man's heart even further. Man found an opportunity in the Law to offer an outward obedience, without any inner transformation.

---

2 Gal 4:1-7
3 Rom 3:21
4 Rom 8:3

Sin is strengthened by the Law!

Only in the context of a humanity that was separated from God, a humanity without intimate relationship with God, was the Law given. The Law, given by God for man's protection, is good in itself. However it created an environment in which sin strengthened itself by the seemingly legitimate distance that the Law maintained. Paul said it this way: "*But sin, that it might appear sin, was producing death in me through what is good, so that sin through the commandment might become exceedingly sinful*" (Rom 7:13) Sin's voice of condemnation is strengthened by the very Law of God that confirms the inadequacy of man to consistently live up to God's standards.

MEDITATION:

When we were minors, we were just like slaves ordered around by simple instructions (the tutors and administrators of this world), with no say in the conduct of our own lives. But when the time arrived that was set by God the Father, God sent his Son, born among us of a woman, born under the conditions of the law so that he might redeem those of us who have been kidnapped by the law. Thus we have been set free to experience our rightful heritage.
Gal 4:3-5 MSG

AFFIRMATION:

I live in the freedom of my rightful heritage: spontaneous, intimate and limitless relationship with God.

Discussion:

- In what context was the Law given?
- Discuss how the Law is a way of relating to God.
- In what way did the Law fall short ... what could it not achieve?

Assignment:

Write a short essay explaining why the law was only a temporal arrangement. Mention what it is, that the Law could not do.

Week 8

God's Strategy with the Law

God did not make a mistake when He gave the Law, neither was He unaware that the Law would in itself not solve the problem of separation. He knew and purposely designed the Law in such a way that it would intensify the conflict - that it would reveal the problem for what it really was and reveal man's impotence to solve the problem by himself. He designed this environment of conflict - a conflict that was working its way towards a climax. "Therefore the law is holy, and the commandment holy and just and good." (Rom 7:12). In its context, it served the purpose of God. Outside of this context it becomes a man-made evil system of oppression.

Under the Law, man and God never met face to face. Instead of direct contact with God, the Law became the intermediary by which man related to God based on a knowledge of good and evil, right and wrong. The Law maintained the distance between God and man and in so doing, prolonged and intensified the conflict.

Although the law was not designed to *solve* the problem of separation, it was designed to *reveal* the problem. The Law revealed another law or government. Paul says that under the Law, he discovered another law or government at work within him. "*For I delight in the law of God according to the inward man. But I see another law in my members, warring against the law of my mind, and bringing me into captivity to the law of sin which is in my members.*" (Rom 7:21,22) The experience of man under the law, was that there was a stronger influence in man that forced him to live contrary to what he knew was right. The flesh became the domain of sin and man by himself was helpless to change the situation. And so Paul continues in verse 23: "*O wretched man that I am! Who will deliver me from this body of death? I thank God—through Jesus Christ our Lord!*"

The fullness of time was drawing near in which the final judgement upon sin and self-righteousness would be complete. "*But when the fullness of the time had come, God sent forth His Son, born of a woman, born under the law, to redeem those who were under the law, that we might receive the adoption as sons.*" Gal 4:4,5

God was preparing to enter the domain of sin - flesh. He was preparing to enter the strong man's house, bind him and spoil his goods. "*For what the law was powerless to do because it was weakened by the flesh, God did by sending his own Son in the likeness of sinful flesh to be a sin offering. And so he condemned sin in the flesh,*" (Rom 8:3) He came to take back every part of humanity that He created, including flesh!

Meditation:

"For what the law was powerless to do because it was weakened by the flesh, God did by sending his own Son in the likeness of sinful flesh to be a sin offering. And so he condemned sin in the flesh,"
Rom 8:3

Affirmation:

I thank God that through Jesus Christ our Lord, He delivered me from the dominion of sin and death.

Discussion:

- What problem did the Law reveal?
- Is the Law system still valid today? (Rom7:6)
- Discuss ways in which people continue to live in the Law-system, even though Christ fulfilled it.

Assignment:

Write a short essay explaining what the law could never do, was done by God in Christ.

Week 9
The Perfect Law of Liberty

The new covenant knows of only one valid law - the law of life in Christ Jesus. This has nothing to do with your effort, self discipline or contribution, but everything to do with discovering yourself, your life, in Christ Jesus.

James calls it the perfect law of liberty. The law of liberty sounds so contradictory. Laws are designed to limit freedom, to restrict movement, to control. But the law of liberty is very different. In verse 1:23 James says that if any man hears this Word he is like a man that sees the face of his birth as in a mirror. Then James continues by saying that the secret of living according to our original design is looking deeply into the perfect law of liberty ... and continuing therein. This law demands that once you see yourself you do whatever you please! God knows that your true self has nothing in itself that is offensive to Him.

The law of life in Christ Jesus, the perfect law of liberty simply states: Know yourself and be yourself. The secret of your life is your union with Christ in God. In Christ Jesus, God and man meet, what 'is' and what 'ought to be' is united and in so doing every difference, every gap, every possible sense of separation is destroyed.

God has no desire to limit or restrain you - His desire is to set you free to be yourself.[1] You are His workmanship, created in Christ Jesus.[2] He is not ashamed to call you His brother, for you share the same origin.[3]

Come on! See who you really are ... and then be who you really are.

1 Gal 5:13
2 Eph 2:10
3 Heb 2:11

MEDITATION:

"But he who looks carefully into the faultless law, the [law] of liberty, and is faithful to it and perseveres in looking into it, being not a heedless listener who forgets but an active doer , he shall be blessed in his doing,"

James 1:25 AMP

AFFIRMATION:

I look deeply into the perfect law of liberty - through it I understand who I am, and that inspires the way I live.

Discussion:

- How does the law of liberty differ from the old Law?
- How does knowing yourself relate to being yourself?

Assignment:

Write a short essay about the freedom you have found in Christ.

Week 10
Incarnation

The word 'incarnation' comes from Latin and simply means to make flesh, or become flesh. The scriptural reference for this concept is John 1:14 "*...and the Word became flesh*"

In every religion and philosophy, word remains word; religion remains a theory and philosophy remains a guess. But in Jesus Christ, the Word is made flesh, reality is revealed - God's thought is concluded in human life. The ultimate destiny of God's Word was never a book or an institution, but flesh ... His image and likeness unveiled in man.

But what is this 'Word' that became flesh. John tells us in the first verse: it is the Word that was in the beginning with God … in fact this 'Word' is God!

[1]Throughout the ages God revealed fragments of His mind. The Old Testament is a record of the many prophets, priests and scholars, scattered throughout many generations, who perceived portions of God's purpose. The best scholars steeped themselves into detailed studies, trying to piece together this puzzle.

Despite the thousands of years of inspired utterance and

1 Heb 1:1

scholastic studies, there remained a mystery which no eye had seen, no ear had heard - a mystery beyond the capability of any imagination![2]

No one except God could ever have conceived such a plan: Eternity would enter time; the infinite would enter space. God would become a man!

The Word, the expression of God, the exact representation of God became flesh! This was no half-hearted attempt by which God simply disguised Himself in a human body. This was a permanent commitment by which God forever joined Himself to humanity - His eternal destiny bound up in the destiny of man. He became man in the fullest sense possible and would remain a man forever.

The authentic Creator, the true light that enlightens every man was coming into this world.[3] His mission was nothing less than shattering our illusions, exposing the unreal, unoriginal and fake identity that we embraced outside of Him. The incarnation reveals that our true selves, our true humanity can only be found in union with God.

When the Word became flesh, when God became a man, it was the Creator and Origin of every man that was made flesh in the person of Christ Jesus. As such He represents

---

2 John 1:18, 1 Cor 2:9
3 John 1:9

each and every man. Everything He did, and everything that happened to Him, happened in the context of the incarnation, the context of a God who so completely embraced His creation, that whatever happened to Him, happened to His creation.

MEDITATION:

The original, authentic Word was face to face with God from the very beginning. God Himself is the content of this communication - revealing His personal presence and unique expression in all that exists.
In fact there is nothing original or innovative outside of Him! He is the only Creator and the source of all inspiration and creativity. Everything that is, has 'Made by God' stamped on its existence.
The life that was in Him was made manifest in man - His life shines in man. (The very life of God is what ignited the existence of man) This original light still shines even in darkness and no amount of darkness can put this light out.
(John 1:1-5 Breath of Life Translation)

AFFIRMATION:

God invented me and gave unique expression to Himself when He created me.

Discussion:

- Discuss what you learned from meditating on John1:1-5
- Discuss the significance of the Creator becoming a creature, of God becoming a man.

Assignment:

Write a short essay explaining the concept of 'incarnation', specifically as it applies to Jesus.

WEEK 11
JESUS - FULLY GOD

Jesus represents God in the fullest, truest sense possible. Jesus not only represents God, He is God. What He says, God says; what He does, God does. Jesus Himself said "if you've seen me, you've seen the Father".[1] Paul wrote in 2 Cor 5:19 that God was in Christ reconciling the world to Himself.

The implications of this incarnation are staggering! God became man without ceasing to be God. Jesus boldly declares "... before Abraham was, I AM."[2] Neither did this transformation, this form of existence as a man, frustrate God. In fact Col 1:19 shows that this was a pleasure! Col 2:9 reveals that God in all His fullness found expression in the body of Christ Jesus! Man is God-compatible!

God does not consider the human body an embarrassment to His desire to reveal and express Himself. He knows that our very existence is the result of His artistic expression to portray His image and likeness. The most accurate and exact reflection of God was revealed in the man Jesus Christ. "*...Jesus is the radiant and flawless expression of the person of God. He makes the glory (intent) of God visible*

1 John 14:9
2 John 8:58

and exemplifies the character and every attribute of God in human form." (Heb 1:3) Christ did not come to bring another dim or obscure view, but a full and complete and crystal clear view of our Father and our likeness to Him. Whatever the Word was in God, before the incarnation, He now is within human form.[3] He was not reduced in person or expressive ability when He became man. He is still the eternal Word, present to God, face to face with God, the mirror image of God, who Himself is God ... and is man. To exist as a man was His plan from the beginning.

So in the person of Christ God gave unhindered expression to Himself and in so doing, revealed what He was really like. Jesus is the revelation of the true identity and character of God. Against a backdrop of rituals and laws and judgements which confused so many about the character of God, He shows up personally to remove every misconception. He is not vengeful - He is willing to take our just punishment upon Himself. He is not easily offended, but rather at the peak of our enmity[4] against Him, He is willing to reconcile us to Himself even while we were still dead in our trespasses and sins.[5]

God is often described in lofty terms such as: Omnipresent (present everywhere); Omniscient (all knowing);

---

3 John 1:14
4 Rom 5:10
5 Eph 2:4

Omnipotent (all powerful). However, in becoming man in Christ Jesus, He limits Himself to a single location; we read that He grew in knowledge and wisdom, and that in His home town He could not do many mighty works because of their unbelief. Despite the fact that Jesus was no longer omnipresent, omniscient or omnipotent, God was still able to fully be Himself in Christ! Why? Because in essence God is love and the human existence is not in any way an inferior expression of His love or life.

He lived fully and continues to express Himself without constraint in the man Christ Jesus! Our humanity is not a constraint to God's ability to fully and freely express Himself. You are not a frustration to God, you are His opportunity to be.

Jesus did not come to change the heart and mind of God concerning man. He came to reveal the truth about God and about us and in so doing make us true - genuinely ourselves.

"*God, who has saved us and called us to a holy life—not because of anything we have done but because of his own purpose and grace. This grace was given us in Christ Jesus before the beginning of time, but it has now been revealed through the appearing of our Savior, Christ Jesus, who has destroyed death and has brought life and immortality to light through the gospel.*" 2 Tim 1:9,10

God's mind and attitude towards us was established before time began. He gave us grace - gave us Himself even before we were born, before we could do anything to deserve it, or not deserve it. Before we had any opportunity to impress or disappoint Him, He was already impressed - impressed with the image and likeness He stamped upon our beings. From His point of view we were found before we were lost - He found us in Christ before He lost us in Adam. We were given grace before the fall. He was simply waiting for the opportune time in which to appear - in which to reveal what has always been: the reality of our salvation in Christ Jesus.

Meditation:

...Jesus is the radiant and flawless expression of the person of God. He makes the glory (intent) of God visible and exemplifies the character and every attribute of God in human form.

Heb 1:3 Mirror Translation

Affirmation:

God demonstrated in Jesus that He is able to be Himself in human form. I am not a frustration to God ... I am His opportunity to be!

Discussion:

- What is the most accurate revelation of God.
- Discuss the fact that God was not limited, reduced or frustrated in the human person of Christ Jesus.

Assignment:

Write a short essay explaining why Jesus is the fullest and final revelation of who God is.

Week 12

Jesus - Fully Man

God became man in the fullest sense possible[1] - He embraced humanity in this act of incarnation to such an extent that all of humanity would be represented in His person.[2] The extent to which He became man, is the extent to which this salvation is reality to us. We were in His life, His death, His resurrection and His ascension. He took humanity upon Himself, within Himself, with such intensity that God would consider His every act as the act of man. His accomplishments would be credited to the account of mankind. He represents man more completely, truly and fully than any other man.

Your birth did not take God by surprise! When you showed up on planet earth, is not when He found out about you. He knew you before you were born[3]. He was intimately acquainted with your design and chose you individually before time began.

What He knew about you before your birth is still His only reference for who you are. Your successes or failures have not changed His mind about you. Love never stops

1 John 1:1,14
2 Rom 5:18, 2 Cor 5:14,19
3 Jer 1:5

believing the best; never stops hoping; never runs out of patience and love never fails.

He knows the truth about you. Eph 1:13 describes this message as the "*word of truth - the gospel of your salvation*" This is the good news of the reality of what God did for you and of what Jesus did on your behalf: He redeemed your original design.

We often read, especially in theological books, about the nature of man. (It's interesting that this term is rarely used in the scriptures.) So I did some research as to what most theologians mean by 'nature of man'. It means the truth or reality of man!

That is such a clear and simple definition - the problem is that many try to find the truth and reality of man in Adam's fall. We should look a bit further back and discover Gen 1:26 - The truth and reality of man came out of God. His nature was the origin of our nature. His reality is the substance we were made from!

The key to understanding the mystery of God-and-man-in-the-one-person-of-Christ, is to realise that He designed man for this very purpose of unity with God. There is no conflict in God's design between the nature of man and the nature of God.

Man is God's idea. And so when God became man it was the original, authentic idea of man that manifested in the person of Christ - the perfect man[4]. What God always knew to be true of man suddenly burst upon the stage of human history. "*The true light that gives light to every man was coming into the world.*" John 1:9 He is the light that reveals the truth about all of humanity, and to each one individually. The revelation He brings is "...full of grace and truth".

The fact that God was able to become man, is testament to the integrity of our design. When He originally created man saying: "*Be our image and our likeness*", He did not create an inferior creature to Himself - He created exactly what he said: His own mirror reflection in form and substance. In Jesus we recognise God as bone of our bone and flesh of our flesh. This likeness is the basis for intimacy without shame and without hindrance.

4 Eph 4:13

MEDITATION:

The Word became flesh
and took up residence in us.
We observed His glory,
the glory of the unique Son from the Father,
full of grace and truth.
John 1:14

AFFIRMATION:

The Word continues to become flesh in me. Lord Jesus live your life through me.

Discussion:

- How did God preserve His design of man? What does Jesus' humanity reveal about man.
- What is the true nature of man?

Assignment:

Write a short essay, exploring the union of God and man in Jesus and what this union reveals about man.

Week 13

God's permanent commitment

The story of Adam and Eve has sometimes been presented as God's first attempts at relationship with man. However the fall forced Him to think of an alternative. That is not true.

The need for the incarnation did not surprise God - He planned this before the fall.[1] The incarnation - the event in which God would become man - was His idea from the start. The fall did not necessitate redemption; redemption was planned before the fall.[2]

He did not simply endure being human for 33 years and then, with great relief, returned to being God! 1 Tim 2:5, was written after the resurrection and ascension and reveals that Christ Jesus is still a man: "*For there is one God and one Mediator between God and men, the Man Christ Jesus*". The incarnation is permanent. He united Himself with Humanity in such a way that He would never be separated again. He bound Himself to our existence; committed Himself to our destiny. The resurrection is proof that this God-man union is not a temporary event, but an eternal unbreakable union.

---

1 Is 46:10
2 2 Tim 1:9

Mediator normally refers to a third party who stands between two other parties - in the gap - in order to make peace or negotiate a deal. However Christ is a completely different type of mediator: God and man meet in this one person of Christ Jesus. He is not a third party; He is God and He is man. This is the perfect mediation in which man faces God directly and God faces man directly and brings about a perfect harmony in the person of Christ.

God has invested everything He has, everything He is, in mankind.[3] He has no other investment, no other interest, no other occupation than you! He believes in you, He is fully committed to you. "*...How many are Your thoughts toward me, how vast the sum of them...*" Ps 139:17

3 Phil 2:7

Meditation:

For there is one God and one Mediator between God and men, the Man Christ Jesus
1 Tim 2:5

Affirmation:

The union of God and man in Christ Jesus, has no distance or separation in it. This is the same union I enjoy: No distance, no separation!

Discussion:

- How does the mediation of Christ differ from any other mediation?
- Discuss the fact that God is still a man in the person of Christ Jesus.

Assignment:

Write a short essay, contrasting the difference between a religion that sees God as separate from ourselves, and what Christ revealed: God and man united in one.

Week 14

All - The scope of God's love.

"... there is one body and one Spirit, just as you were called in one hope of your calling; one Lord, one faith, one baptism; one God and Father of all, who is above all, and through all, and in all. But to each one of us grace was given according to the measure of Christ's gift." Eph 4:4-7

Notice the following from the scripture above: " *...Father of ALL... above ALL ... through ALL ... in ALL ... but to EACH ONE of us grace was given*"

In this lesson, we'll look at the scope of God's love, and in the next lesson we'll look at the focus of His love. Both are important and compliment one another. If we give a wrong emphasis to personal encounter it can become so narrow-minded, so introspective that it excludes and becomes useless to humanity. In the same way, we can so focus on the all-inclusive nature of redemption that it becomes theoretical and without personal impact.

The gospel reveals that God has successfully reconciled all to Himself, with such intensity that each one is called by name into a personal encounter with God. This very individual encounter does not exclude humanity, but invites them into the same unique and deeply personal relationship with Him.

Who is God's audience, and who benefits from what He has done?

The word 'all' is very prevalent in Paul's writings. This has presented great difficulties to those who hold to a theory of 'some' are elected and 'some' are rejected. One of the arguments that they present to counter the meaning of the word 'all' is that Paul obviously wrote to a specific audience of believers and that the 'all' he spoke of, is limited to the people he wrote to.

Well, thankfully Paul himself gave us an explanation of what he meant when he said 'all'.

Col 1:15-20
"He is the image of the invisible God, the firstborn over ALL creation. For by Him ALL things were created that are in heaven and that are on earth, visible and invisible, whether thrones or dominions or principalities or powers. ALL things were created through Him and for Him. And He is before ALL things, and in Him ALL things consist. And He is the head of the body, the church, who is the beginning, the firstborn from the dead, that in ALL things He may have the preeminence.

For it pleased the Father that in Him ALL the fullness should dwell, and by Him to reconcile ALL things to Himself, by Him, whether things on earth or things in heaven, having made peace through the blood of His cross."

So Paul defines what 'all' means, namely: everything created, visible or invisible. There is only one Creator, and everything He created is the audience of reconciliation.

Again in Rom 5:18 Paul gives a clear definition of what he means by all.

"Therefore, as through one man's offense judgment came to ALL men, resulting in condemnation, even so through one Man's righteous act the free gift came to ALL men, resulting in justification of life."

Obviously Paul is not limiting his use of the word 'all' to those who first received the letter. Yes, he wrote the letter to a specific audience, but his message concerns all men in all time. In fact, on one occasion Paul says that he is a minister to all of creation under heaven! (Col 1:23)

A scripture that summarises the all-inclusive work of Christ is 2 Cor 5:19: "*...in Christ, God was reconciling the world to Himself, not counting their trespasses against them, and He has committed the message of reconciliation to us."*

Even the classic passages (Rom 9-11) that were used to support the idea of 'some' are elect and 'some' are rejected, end with this conclusion: "For God has imprisoned ALL in disobedience, so that He may have mercy on ALL." (Rom 11:32)

If you read all three chapters in context, you'll notice that the 'elect' become the 'non-elect' and the 'non-elect' become the 'elect'. Being non-elect therefore is not a permanent state that cannot be changed, rather it is a temporal state, to which there is only one ultimate conclusion. The message translation says it so beautifully:

"*...there was a time not so long ago when you were on the outs with God. But then the Jews slammed the door on him and things opened up for you. Now they are on the outs. But with the door held wide open for you, they have a way back in. In one way or another, God makes sure that we ALL experience what it means to be outside so that he can personally open the door and welcome us back in.*" Rom 11:30-32 MSG

It is clear, all means all. The scope of what Christ did for man is all-inclusive – the world was reconciled, the world was forgiven.

MEDITATION:

For it pleased the Father that in Him ALL the fullness should dwell, and by Him to reconcile ALL things to Himself, by Him, whether things on earth or things in heaven, having made peace through the blood of His cross.

Col 1:19,20

AFFIRMATION:

God successfully reconciled all, giving me the boldness to approach anyone, knowing that He makes His appeal through me.

Discussion:

- Who did God reconcile to Himself?
- Discuss what it means for God to make His appeal through us.

Assignment:

Write a short essay showing how both Adam and Jesus represented all of humanity.

Week 15

Each - The focus of His love

Within the enormity and all-inclusive nature of this redemption, God preserved His focus and the intensity of its implications for each individual. As the Message translation states so beautifully:
"*God doesn't count us; he calls us by name.*
Arithmetic is not his focus. " Rom 9:27

God is not a duplicator, but a creator. He uniquely and individually designed you. You were on His mind from the beginning.
"*Even as [in His love] He chose us [actually picked us out for Himself as His own] in Christ before the foundation of the world, that we should be holy (consecrated and set apart for Him) and blameless in His sight, even above reproach, before Him in love.*"
Eph 1:4 Amp

His love is not a general feeling of goodwill towards humanity, but an intense love which began even before time began, when He dreamed about you individually. He knew you even before He formed you in your mother's womb.[1]

---

1 Jer 1:5

O LORD, You have searched me and known me.
You know when I sit down and when I rise up;
You understand my thought from afar.
You scrutinize my path and my lying down,
And are intimately acquainted with all my ways.
Even before there is a word on my tongue,
Behold, O LORD, You know it all.
You have enclosed me behind and before,
And laid Your hand upon me.

My frame was not hidden from You,
When I was made in secret,
And skillfully wrought in the depths of the earth;
Your eyes have seen my unformed substance;
And in Your book were all written
The days that were ordained for me,
When as yet there was not one of them.
(Ps 139:1-5,15,16)

Can it get more personal, more intimate than that? He knew you, dreamt about you, and anticipated every detail of your life, before you were formed!

At one stage Jesus asked His disciples: "Who do people say that the Son of Man is?" They answered: "Some say John the Baptist; others say Elijah; and others Jeremiah or one of the prophets."[2]

2 Mat 16:13-16

For many of us, there was a time where we only knew Jesus based on what someone told us about Him. And there are many opinions to choose from. But there comes a time when He confronts you personally and says: "But who do you say that I am?"

His knowledge of you is not general … He even knows the number of hairs you have on your head! He desires that your knowledge of Him will also be just as personal and intimate.

The intensity of the incarnation.
When the Word became flesh, the implications were both universal and individual. He embraced humanity and your being individually. He made your cause His own. You were present, when your Creator, your Designer, your Originator became a man in the person of Christ Jesus.

The relationship between God and man was fulfilled, completed and perfected in this one God-man person, Christ Jesus. We are invited into an already perfected relationship. "God is faithful, by whom you were called into the fellowship of His Son, Jesus Christ our Lord."
1 Cor 1:9

This does not simply refer to fellowship with Jesus, but the fellowship of Jesus. In other words the same quality of fellowship Jesus enjoys with the Father, is the quality of relationship you are called into.

Love anticipates a response of equal quality … love aims to awaken and stir.
"*As for me, I will continue beholding Your face in righteousness; I shall be fully satisfied, when I awake beholding Your likeness*" Ps 17:15
This is part of what repentance means: to come to your senses, to come to yourself, to awaken!

We can make a decision for God, because He made one for us. We love, because He first loved us. We can respond in faith as we reflect the faith He has shown in us. This romance, this ecstasy has no place for formal protocols and mechanical replies … simply respond naturally to the love He reveals.

In conclusion: The scope of God's love is 'all', the focus of His love is each one. Understanding the 'all' gives us the motivation to speak to any person. In our communication of the gospel, the aim is nothing less than bringing the individual to a place of intimate encounter with God. To do that we need to see both these aspects: this person is included … part of the 'all' and secondly, this person is individually known and loved by God. What good news!

Meditation:

My frame was not hidden from You,
When I was made in secret,
And skillfully wrought in the depths of the earth;
Your eyes have seen my unformed substance;
And in Your book were all written
The days that were ordained for me,
When as yet there was not one of them.
Ps 139:15,16

Affirmation:

He intimately knew me before He formed me. I was personally included in Christ - I am the focus of His love.

Discussion:

- Each share a short testimony of how you personally realised who Christ is.

Assignment:

Write a short essay describing the individual and intimate relationship God desires, as displayed in Jesus Christ.

Week 16
Word became Flesh

The Word became flesh. (John 1:14) John chooses the word flesh. He could have said *the word became man*, but he chooses the word *flesh*. Why? Of all the attributes of man, our intellect, our social interaction, our spirituality, flesh is the most base. Flesh represented the arena of conflict, the environment in which temptation thrived. Flesh became the domain of sin. Jesus becomes man in every respect because only that which He becomes, can be saved.

Jesus did not arrive on this earth with supernatural protection against the evil that plagues humanity. It was into this domain of conflict, into our humanity with all its contradictions, temptation and weakness that Christ entered. The reign of death, the bondage and the curse introduced by Adam and the consequent righteous judgement of God, was the human condition into which Christ was born. And so Paul writes: "*But when the fullness of the time had come, God sent forth His Son, born of a woman, born under the law, to redeem those who were under the law, that we might receive the adoption as sons.*"[1]

The true light entered the kingdom of darkness and refused to be dimmed or put out. The true man entered fallen

1 Gal. 4:4,5 NKJV

humanity but refused to submit to the lie of a lesser identity. He knew that sin was not an attribute of true humanity, but an attribute of inhumanity. He entered a humanity at enmity against God, but refused to allow His view and knowledge of God to be perverted, refused to see God as the enemy. He brings the conflict to a climax and in so doing, He condemns sin in the flesh. "*For what the law could not do in that it was weak through the flesh, God did by sending His own Son in the likeness of sinful flesh, on account of sin: He condemned sin in the flesh*" [2]

He fully identified with fallen man, fully subjected himself to the battles with which sinful man struggled ... yet He remained sinless. The baptism of John was a baptism of repentance - that is why John objected to Christ being baptised. But the baptism of repentance was part of Christ representing man, identifying Himself with sinful man and repenting on their behalf. This was part of Christ fulfilling all righteousness - meeting the righteous demands made upon man under the law.

It is in the very act of becoming flesh that the redemption of the flesh begins, that the dominance of sin was broken and man was restored to liberty and freedom from a foreign ruler. He becomes the last Adam; He brings to

---

2 Rom 8:3 NKJV

an end the dominion of sin and death in man. By His perfect obedience within this flesh, He exposes the lie of the kingdom of darkness and brings to a final end the race of humanity that lived in subjection to this false identity. In so doing He becomes the firstborn of the new creation. The first man in whom God is not frustrated or limited by flesh, but in Christ the fullness of the Godhead dwells in bodily form.[3]

Let's summarise before we move on. Redemption is not a specific act in the life of Jesus - it can't be limited to His death or any other event, but rather it begins and is completed within the incarnation. His death, resurrection and ascension (to which we will give more attention later) are all part of, and happen within the context of the incarnation, of the God-man union in the person of Christ.

3 Col 2:9

MEDITATION:

For in him dwelleth all the fulness of the Godhead bodily. And ye are complete in him
Col 2:9,10

AFFIRMATION:

I am His workmanship, designed by Him and for Him. My body is not an obstacle for Him, but His opportunity to live and move and have His being in this world, in bodily form!

Discussion:

- Discuss the significance of Jesus overcoming sin as a man (Rom 8:3) and what that means to you.
- Discuss the significance of the incarnation being the context in which Christ Jesus lived, died and rose again.

Assignment:

Write a short essay discussing the incarnation as the context in which Christ Jesus lived, died and rose again.

Week 17
Pictures of Redemption

The Old testament mainly uses three words to describe redemption. There is an obvious overlap in the meaning of these words, but each of them also has a distinct emphasis.

1. Padah

The first Hebrew word we'll examine is *padah.*

When this word is used, the emphasis is usually on the cost of redemption and the nature of the act of redemption. Interestingly the object of redemption is always a living thing and so the substitutionary idea of 'a life for a life' developed.

The primary use of *padah* is in relation to the redemption of Israel out of Egypt.[1]

Padah is used to describe the redemption of God's people, God's property, out of an oppressive alien power and out of the judgement of God. Israel's redemption included both a deliverance from Egypt - the alien power - as well as from the angel of death which was sent by God.

---

1 Ex 13:14, Deut 9:26; 13:5, 15:15

At no time is there any hint of a ransom paid to the enemy. God did not bargain with Egypt or pay a ransom for Israel, because Israel never belonged to Egypt!

2. Kipper, kopher (redeem, ransom)

Kipper is used to describe redemption in terms of the act of wiping out sin or debt; to nullify its effect by the provision of a sacrifice. It is used both in the context of the law[2] and within the context of the priestly rituals of atoning sacrifices.

The judgement of God has been misunderstood by many. However, in order to understand redemption, we need to understand judgement. God's righteous judgement is not an attribute in contradiction to His love - God is not in conflict with Himself. His just judgement is as much part of His love as His forgiveness.

God's wrath and judgement is against anything that brings separation, against anything that tries to reduce the pure and intimate relationship He designed, to something less. It is exactly because He loves man that He judges sin. His judgement is not against true man as such, but against anything that would reduce man to less than His original design. God will not settle for an inferior relationship.

However, man is responsible for allowing, or inviting the

2 Ex 21:28-30

separation, responsible for choosing an alternative and lesser way of life. As such, man took within himself that which is subject to God's righteous judgement. Man has no means by which to atone or provide a sacrifice that will satisfy this justice.

But God devised a way in which He could be both just and the justifier of men; a way in which He could judge sin completely and destroy its separating effect without destroying man. He provides the atoning sacrifice for man and thereby reconciles man back to Himself. He both judges and forgives in the same act. Atonement is not a way of covering the face of God so that He does not notice sin. No! It's God's way of covering and protecting man while He judges sin and destroys it.

This made the sacrificial system of Israel different from all other cults. The pagan sacrifices were meant to appease their gods. However, the Old Covenant sacrifices were commissioned by God - it was His initiative to atone for and save His people from their sins. God provides the atonement![3]

3. Gaal, goel (redeem, redeemer)

The focus here is primarily on the nature of the redeemer. It has a rich and beautiful background in the family-property law, referring to redemption out of bankruptcy or bondage

3 Deut 21:8; Ps 65:3

by a kinsman (relation) who is bound to the person in trouble both in blood and in the community of property.

When the verb *gaal* is used, it means to lay claim on something that has been lost or forfeited. When the noun *goel* is used, it describes the claimant who on the basis of a relationship of responsibility, qualifies as the redeemer. The object of redemption can either be property or a person who has sold themselves into slavery. The book of Ruth is the best example of this in the Old Testament.

… *The Reality of Redemption in Christ* …

These pictures give us such beautiful insight into our redemption in Christ Jesus. Jesus comes to this world as the rightful owner and as mankind's next of kin. He comes as one bound to humanity, already in relationship with humanity because of our common origin;[4] He comes to lay claim on His own; He comes claiming our cause as His own. His relationship with humanity is demonstrated in the most fundamental way as He becomes flesh of our flesh and bone of our bone.

It's interesting to note that those who are redeemed, do not become related to the redeemer after redemption, or when they accept redemption. Redemption is only possible because the redeemer is already related to those whom he redeems! Our redemption in Christ Jesus is predicated on

4 Heb 2:11, Acts 17:26

the fact that He is related to mankind - we have the same origin.

Mankind belongs to God. Evil never had a legitimate claim on, or ownership of man. Redemption in Christ Jesus includes both a deliverance from an alien oppressive power as well as deliverance from the just judgement of God against sin. And this redemption comes at the highest price.

When the uniquely begotten son of God becomes flesh, He takes on humanity's cause as His own. He faces the alien power not as a remote God, but He enters the arena of conflict, fully identified with man's slavery and weakness. Jesus faces temptation, in which His identity is questioned. He is given every opportunity to question God and is offered the opportunity to submit to an alternative authority (Matt 4), but He refuses. Even though He was born of a woman, part of the race under the curse of Adam's disobedience, He refuses this false identity. He remains perfectly obedient to the only rightful authority and because of His perfect obedience He condemns this lesser identity in the flesh thereby opening the way for us to once again be our true selves.

In Rom 7 Paul speaks about man's condition under the law; he speaks about this alien force or government within him that forced him to do what he did not want to do. This is slavery to sin, slavery to a way of thinking and consequently a way of acting that is far inferior to our original design. But even in this state, Paul still acknowledges that sin is not a natural attribute of man, but something separate from him, yet present within him. Despite man's best efforts, the conclusion is clear: man is powerless to free himself, to redeem himself.

This reminds me of what Jesus said about entering a strong man's house. (Matt 22:29) Sin found a home in human flesh and became a strong and enslaving presence. However, a stronger man entered the house and bound sin, spoiling his goods! Christ entered the human body and condemned sin in flesh. Sin has no independent power or influence outside of your co-operation and consent. A stronger one has come and has given the opportunity for us to reign and rule in life, even in our body of flesh. This flesh body has now become the temple, the dwelling place of the Most High God!

MEDITATION:

Because both he who carried out the act of rescue and those whom he rescued and restored to innocence originate from the same source, he proudly introduces them as members of his immediate family.
Heb 2:11 Mirror Translation

AFFIRMATION:

Jesus is my kinsman redeemer - He came and made my cause His own, uniting Himself with me. He is for me, who can be against me!

Discussion:

- What was the cost of redemption.
- Discuss the act of redemption.
- Discuss the nature of the kinsman redeemer.

Assignment:

Write a short essay about the kinsman redeemer and how that relates to Jesus' relationship with humanity.

Week 18
At-one-ment

Jesus reveals the God who is with us in all the contradiction and conflict, the God who is present even in pain, the One who understands you better than what you understand yourself, for He is not observing you from a distance, He experiences everything you experience. He knows your sitting down and your standing up, your every thought before you think it, your every word before you say it. He is intimately acquainted with all your ways.

Ultimately, in the person of Jesus Christ, the all-knowing, all powerful and all-present God, willingly lays down these divine privileges, subjecting Himself to our uncertainties, our limitations and confines Himself to a human body … in one person, in one place. He fully identifies with us. He does all of this without ceasing to be God!

This identification culminates on the cross. This is where an immortal God will face death; where God Himself will feel what it is like to be godforsaken!

Jesus, taking upon Himself the mindset of fallen humanity, partakes even of our doubt and cries out: "My God, My God, why have you forsaken me?"

He shows the unshakable nature of his faith, not by avoiding our doubt, but by assuming our doubt and crying out on our behalf. He then proceeds to answer that question Himself, by descending into the deepest despair, the domain of evil itself, and in the midst of it all, He shows that God is still present. "For He has not despised or detested the torment of the afflicted. He did not hide His face from him but listened when he cried to Him for help" (Ps 22:24 HCSB)

For he hath made him to be sin for us, who knew no sin; that we might be made the righteousness of God in him. 2 Cor 5:21

In the same way in which He became sin (without personally sinning) so that we might become the righteousness of God, He fully faced and assumed our doubt, so that we might become partakers of His faith.

Jesus did not just solve our problems by waving a magic wand from afar. He entered into the middle of the conflict, stepped into the domain of contradiction, entered our hell, faced death itself and from there He conquered. Atonement is His at-one-ment with us. The early church fathers said it this way: "What is unassumed is unhealed, but whatever He becomes, He saves"

He demonstrates the integrity of His peace, not by avoiding

our problems, but by embracing all of humanity with all of our problems and issues, without loosing His peace.

He knows you, He understands you better than you understand yourself. He is fully aware of every details of your life ... and He loves you. He is not uninvolved or unaware. The incarnation is the event in which God demonstrates His union with your humanity, with all its challenges and contradiction ... bringing His peace to you, no matter what circumstances you find yourself in.

He demonstrates the robustness of His life, not by avoiding death, but by entering into the heart of it, and there in the midst of the greatest contradiction He bursts forth into resurrection life.

Meditation:

"For He has not despised or detested the torment of the afflicted. He did not hide His face from him but listened when he cried to Him for help" (Ps 22:24 HCSB)

Affirmation:

I am never alone. God defined himself as the God who is with me!

Discussion:

- What does atonement mean?
- What does this say about the character of God?

Assignment:

Write a short essay on the extend to which God has made himself one with you.

Week 19
Resurrection

There are two sides to justification. On one side, it is the just judgement of sin and on the other side, it is the vindication of man. "*He who was delivered over because of our transgressions, and was raised because of our justification.*" (Rom 4:25 NAS)

The resurrection is God's undisputed declaration that man is righteous! Just as His death was the final 'No!' to the alternative man, so His resurrection is the ultimate 'Yes!' to the original man. It is the vindication and final victory of God's authentic design of man. His death brought the conflict between these options to a climax; His resurrection is the end of all conflict, the demonstration of His victory.[1]

All contradiction between God and man, came to an end in the resurrection. This means that God's reality is now available to us.[2] His truth which is beyond dispute or contradiction is accessible for us to live in. His Word did not return to Him void, but accomplished what He purposed. The gap between heaven and earth, His thoughts and our thoughts, His reality and our reality, has been

1 Eph 2:14-18
2 Col 3:1

bridged. As He is, so are we in this world!

God's love dream did not only involve removing everything that abhorred Him, but also included the restoration of the beauty and glory of all that He adores and desires. In His resurrection, mankind was restored to the blameless innocence and beauty that He loves. Our innocence is so much more than the absence of sin, it is the purity and vibrancy of being truly ourselves - our born-of-God selves. It is standing in the simplicity of our true and authentic design, fully satisfied and without any thought of an alternative existence.

The resurrection is more than just another event that follows the event of His death. Jesus said "*I am the resurrection and the life*" (John 11:25) The resurrection is Jesus Christ being Himself - living in the full reality of how God always intended for man to live. A life without any consciousness of sin, not even a consciousness of good and evil, but simply a consciousness of union with the Father. Resurrection life is a life of reigning, where the only memory of an enemy, is a memory of victory.

Meditation:

Pursue with diligence the consequence of your co-inclusion in Christ. Relocate yourself mentally! His resurrection co-raised you to the same position of authority, seated in the strength of God's right hand.
Becoming affectionately acquainted with Throne Room thoughts will keep you from being distracted again by the earthly (soul-ruled) realm.
Col 3:1,2 Mirror Translation

Affirmation:

I was co-raised, co-seated with Christ. The Throne Room is not my destination, but my starting point!

Discussion:

- Discuss how the resurrection is the full manifestation of who Jesus is.
- Discuss the implications of the fact that we were included in His resurrection.

Assignment:

Write a short essay describing what resurrection life is, focussing on victory over the enemy and death.

WEEK 20 RESURRECTION LIFE NOW

The resurrection is a creative event in which the physical body of Jesus was restored, re-created and made fit for life once again. Resurrection is not only some abstract spiritual concept, but a life to be lived in the flesh! This is the greatest demonstration that God does not consider the human body as an obstacle to His life, but a vehicle through which to express it.

The incarnation is permanent! God has made a final choice concerning His preferred form of existence. He chose to become a man and He chose to remain a man, for in man He finds unrestrained expression.[1]

Rom 5:17 describes this resurrection life as one of reigning and ruling in life. Rom 6:11 describes it as unbroken or interrupted fellowship! "*Even so consider yourselves also dead to sin and your relation to it broken, but alive to God [living in unbroken fellowship with Him] in Christ Jesus.*" (Rom 6:11 AMP).

The implications of the resurrection are not concealed for

1 Col 1:19; 2:9

a future day when you die! His death means that newness of life is available to us, now! The rest of Romans 6 shows how this life in the flesh is now an opportunity for God, rather than a struggle with sin.

God entangled with His creation

I'm so glad our faith is not dependant upon scientific fact, but upon a God who reveals Himself. Science, no matter how complimentary it is of our faith, is not meant to prove our faith, or be the basis of our faith. However, it can most definitely confirm our faith.

There are many great resources and youtube videos that explain the science behind 'entanglement' or 'non-locality' in detail. The following is a very basic explanation of it:

If two electrons originate from the same source, they are entangled. One of these electrons can be sent to the other side of the universe, but somehow they will still be connected! Do something to one, and the other electron responds instantly. This has already been proved experimentally over distances of more than 100KM.

We know of nothing that travels faster than light, yet here is proof of a dimension that connects objects without any restraint in space or time. One scientist described it as follows:

Gisin speculates that some "influence" may be affecting both experiments coming from "outside space and time." Gisin says he means by this that "there is no story in space and time" to account for nonlocality. (http://www.informationphilosopher.com/solutions/scientists/gisin/)

In reality these electrons are still entangled … or connected. Everything has a common origin and so, in reality everything is still connected … is still touching!

Another strange fact of this sub-atomic world, is that even the act of observation, changes the state of what is being observed.

So what does all of this have to do with the resurrection of Christ Jesus?
Well, Adam, the crown of creation, through one act of disobedience, entangled all of reality into a downwards spiral of decay and corruption.[2]

The only One who knew the original parameters and state of all creation is the Originator, the Creator. In Christ Jesus, God becomes entangled and intimately connected with His creation. He is absolutely consistent … the decay and the affect of the fall does not change Him … He changes it! His incarnation, His entanglement with our reality, is

2 Rom 8:20

the beginning of the "reconciliation of all things" as Paul words it in Col 1:20.

Paul describes the extent of Christ's entanglement with creation as follows: "*All things were created through Him and for Him. And He is before all things, and in Him all things consist.*" Col 1:17

But the explosive event of the resurrection is where the true power of this entanglement, this connection with creation becomes most visible. This is the birth of the new creation. This is where God manifests Himself in such clarity and purity, with the affect that everything connected with Him, immediately changes state and direction.

As Adam entangled all of creation in a downward spiral of decay, the resurrection of Christ entangled all of creation. He changed the direction and of "*the increase of His government and of peace there shall be no end*" Is 9:7

What is our contribution to this new creation? Well, long before we knew that observation changes things, the scriptures said: "... we continue to behold as in a mirror the glory of the Lord, are constantly being transfigured into His very own image" 2 Cor 3:18

What we perceive, changes what is seen.

Meditation:

Even so consider yourselves also dead to sin and your relation to it broken, but alive to God [living in unbroken fellowship with Him] in Christ Jesus.
Rom 6:11 AMP.

Affirmation:

I have come to this conclusion (reckon myself) that I am indeed dead to sin; I have no relation with it anymore because that relationship died when I died with Christ. I have also concluded this: I was included in His resurrection. That means His life is now my life.

Discussion:

- Discuss the fact that resurrection life is available now!
- What does it mean to 'reckon yourself dead to sin and alive to God'. On what basis can you do that?
- Discuss Col 1:17

Assignment:

Write a short essay celebrating the resurrection of Christ and how this event was the beginning of the new creation.

Week 21
New Reality

When Jesus washed His disciples feet, He humbled Himself in this act of servanthood without losing His dignity or value.[1] When you are secure in the knowledge of your identity, then humbling yourself in servanthood becomes much easier, for far from reducing your identity, such deeds confirm the surety and immutability of your true identity.

Philippians 2 describes the incarnation as an act in which God humbled Himself and took the form of a servant. God Himself, became a servant to mankind! Yet, He was not reduced in person or dignity. He became man without ceasing to be God in any way.

In this sense the ascension is the inverse of the incarnation. The ascension is the glorification of Christ and of man in Christ. It is the act in which God honours Christ and in so doing restores man to the place and position of glory that He intended for us from the beginning. For just as surely as mankind was included in the death and resurrection of Christ, so we were included in His ascension.

The ascension is the act in which man is elevated again

1 John 13

to the place of union with God. Just as God became man without ceasing to be God, so man has been united with God without ceasing to be man. Union with God does not consume man, but rather it releases man to be truly man. We remain distinctly human in union with God.

The Word that was in the beginning, even before space and time, entered our reality but remained the God beyond the limits of space and time. In the ascension we are transported to this eternal realm beyond the limits of space and time, but we also remain in this world in order to redeem time and give God space in this earthly realm.

... Where? ...

"Pursue with diligence the consequence of your co-inclusion in Christ. Relocate yourself mentally! His resurrection co-raised you to the same position of authority, seated in the strength of God's right hand.
Becoming affectionately acquainted with Throne Room thoughts will keep you from being distracted again by the earthly (soul-ruled) realm.

Your union with His death broke the association with that world; the secret of your life now is the fact that you are wrapped up with Christ in God.

Every time Christ is revealed as our life, we are being

co-revealed in the same glory (likeness and image of God) being united together with Him."
(Col 3:1-4 Mirror Translation)

The right-hand of God, a place of authority far above this earthly realm, is now our home-ground! This is the new reality we have to become acquainted with.

This place cannot be accurately described in terms of space and time, for it is the eternal realm beyond the limits of space and time. Eph 4:10 says that he descended and ascended so that He might fill all things. "*He Who descended is the same as He Who also has ascended high above all the heavens, that He might fill all things*". Created time and space has been invaded by the Creator Himself - He fills both creation and the realm beyond creation.

This eternal realm is not far from each one of us, for the limits of space and time are all around us. In Him we live and move and have our being.
Where is the throne room?
Where is this heavenly place?
Wherever Christ is!
For Christ is the place and the moment where God and man encounter each other face to face, without division, separation or confusion.

MEDITATION:

Your union with His death broke the association with that world; the secret of your life now is the fact that you are wrapped up with Christ in God.
Every time Christ is revealed as our life, we are being co-revealed in the same glory (likeness and image of God) being united together with Him."
Col 3:3-4 Mirror Translation

AFFIRMATION:

There is no distance between God and myself. He is in me and I am in Him. I am His location on earth - through me He is able to bring heavenly realities to earth.

Discussion:

- Discuss the implications of union with God.
- What does it mean to be co-revealed with Him?

Assignment:

Write a short essay exploring the meaning of being co-raised with Him. Explore the implications of being seated with Him in heavenly places.

Week 22
Introducing a person to Christ

What does it mean to introduce someone to Christ?
We would never have had the motivation or desire to travel, to minister or share this gospel, if all we had to offer was another opinion or some emotional religious experience. Seeing people come into a living relationship with Christ through the declaration of this gospel, is the greatest privilege there is. Talking about God has little appeal for us ... but allowing God Himself to make His appeal through us is an experience beyond comparison.

So here are a few aspects that I am aware of, and I believe will be helpful to you, when introducing people to Christ:

1. God of initiative.
I'm so glad we are not dealing with a distant, angry God - One who suspiciously looks at your every thought and action to see if you are worthy of meeting with Him. No! Our God - God as revealed in Jesus Christ - took the initiative to meet with us. And His initiative was not limited to taking the first step. He went all the way in reconciling us to Himself. That means that everything that stood between man and God, every offense, every sin, He dealt with.

So introducing someone to Christ is in the first place not focused on what this person needs to do, say, pray or feel, but instead it is based on what God has done! "*Embracing what God does for you is the best thing you can do for him.*" Rom 12:2 MSG

2. The God who is near.

There is nothing more attractive than an awareness of the personal presence of God. What confidence we can have when speaking to people, knowing that the One we speak of, is sustaining their very existence! He upholds them even while they are ignorant of Him. Every cell and atom in their body exists through Him and for Him.[1]

No wonder Paul speaks to unbelieving heathens in Acts 17 and even before they are able to respond or accept his message, Paul says: '*He is not far from each one of us … In Him we live and move and have our being ... for you are indeed His offspring*'!!

"*Let all men know your gentleness and thereby recognise and become aware of the nearness of the Lord.*" Phil 4:5

In Jesus Christ, God demonstrated the union between Himself and man as He always intended it to be. In this

---

1 1Cor 8:6, Col 1:16,17, Heb 1:3

union there is no distance of any kind between man and God. We bring an awareness of the nearness, the closeness of God through the preaching of the gospel. Such an awareness, is faith. Faith is being aware of what God is aware of.

3. Spirit-encounter.

When we introduce Christ to a person, it is in the first instance not a physical, emotional or intellectual introduction, but a spirit-encounter with spirit-reality. Yes, this encounter will affect your emotions, your intellect and your physical existence, but its source is spiritual.[2]

Remember, God was before time and space came into existence. As we saw previously, He sustains all of creation, but we should never allow our concept of Him to be reduced to someone that can be explained or grasped in physical terms. In other words, He does fill all of creation, but He is not contained or limited by creation.

I say this because we have often allowed our understanding of 'introducing Christ' to be reduced to a physical description. God's being and the spirit realm in which He operates is a reality of infinitely greater substance than the physical. That is why some of Jesus' sayings completely challenge our understanding of time and space. For instance, He said: "Before Abraham was, I AM" In our linear understanding

2 1 Cor 2:1-6

of time, this statement would be grammatically incorrect. On another occasion He said: "*In that day you will know that I am in My Father, and you in Me, and I in you.*"[3] In our three-dimensional understanding of space, this saying does not make sense. Three entities occupying the same space simultaneously ... being both the container and the contents ... does not make sense ... in the physical.

When we declare this gospel, we can have confidence that something much wiser than human logic, and something more mysterious than supernatural signs is happening in the hearers. We have all the reason in the world to expect God to reveal Himself! Expect Spirit-encounter beyond the five physical senses; expect God to reveal through His spirit what "*eye has not seen and ear has not heard and has not entered into the heart of man*"[4]

What does this Spirit encounter reveal? "*Now we have received the ... Spirit Who is from God, that we might realise and comprehend and appreciate the gifts and blessing so freely and lavishly bestowed on us by God.*"

Paul once recounted what Jesus commissioned him to do as follows: "*I now send you, to open their eyes, in order to turn them from darkness to light, and from the power of Satan to God, that they may receive forgiveness of sins and*

3 John 14:20
4 1 Cor 2:9

an inheritance among those who are sanctified by faith in Me." (Acts 26:18)

What does it mean for a person to accept Christ other than to 'open their eyes'; to turn from darkness to light! And in opening their eyes they receive and realise what has been freely given to them.

4. Meet yourself!

In meeting Christ Jesus, we meet the One who designed us, planned us, chose us and intimately knows us. We might have much to learn about Him, but He knows everything about us … and much of what can be learnt about Him will be found in what He knows about us. Christ always reveals Himself "as in a mirror", not as a separate entity. (2 Cor 3:18) He reveals Himself as the secret of your true life. (Col 3:3,4) So when you meet Christ, you meet yourself for the very first time! You meet the Author and Perfecter of your design.

What this means in practical terms is that when I speak to someone about Christ, there is no conflict between speaking about who Christ is and speaking about who He made them to be. James says that whenever this word is heard, it is like a man seeing the face of his birth as in a mirror! (James 1:23)

This encounter is described so beautifully in Ps 17:15: "*As for me, I will continue beholding Your face in righteousness; I shall be fully satisfied, when I awake in Your likeness*".

To recognise the Lordship of Jesus Christ cannot be separated from recognising His image and likeness within you. You belong to Him because He made you … and redeemed you! Awake to His reality; awake to His likeness in you!

You are part of God's gift … to you! Unwrap yourself, discover yourself, accept yourself and be thankful for such a thoughtful gift.

MEDITATION:

He is not far from each one of us; for in Him we live and move and exist ...
Acts 17:27,28

AFFIRMATION:

God is able and eager to reveal Himself through me, to unveil the truth of His closeness and His love. I know the truth about every other person ... that is why they are attracted to me. Through me they can discover the truth about themselves.

Discussion:

- Discuss Paul's message to the unbelievers in Athens. Acts 17
- How does Paul's approach differ from what you have witnessed in the past?

Assignment:

Write a short essay describing how introduction a person to Christ is simultaneously an introduction to their own true identity.

Week 23
Faith

In Christ Jesus, mankind is confronted with the reality of our salvation.[1] The message of Christ in nothing less than the unveiling of God's reality - the truth as He sees it. What Christ accomplished is not potentially real or theoretically real or only legally valid, it is simply real!

He is the ultimate representation of the reality of God[2] and the ultimate representation of the reality of man. What He accomplished is nothing less than the reconciliation of God and man. You were in Christ, in His death, in His resurrection and in His Ascension. In Christ you are confronted with the reality of your salvation.

When the Word became flesh, when God became a man, When the Creator became part of creation, He bound Himself inseparably to us. Our existence was changed by this act! We can no longer think of ourselves apart from this event, neither can we think of God apart from His initiative in becoming one with man.

His death was our death. Our guilt and sin met their final end, their final judgement when we died together with

---

1 1 Tim 4:10, Eph 1:13
2 Heb 1:2,3

Christ. The relationship between man and sin was severed in His death and our slate was wiped clean. Every accusation that stood against us and the debt we owed was justly paid in full. The past, with all its guilt and imperfections, was consumed in this death!

We were raised together with Christ. We were restored to the men and women He had in mind since the beginning - the pure and blameless companions He imagined. We are free to be our true selves, without conflict or contradiction! In His resurrection we were restored and translated into God's reality - the kingdom of light. Time itself has been redeemed as God and man meet face to face in the resurrected Jesus Christ. He is eternally present - the new reality of my existence.

Not only were we united with God in his death and resurrection, but we were raised with Him into heavenly places. The ascension is the glorification of man to the place and position that He prepared for us - permanent union with Him.

All of this is of God, He accomplished it without our help and without our permission! It is truth whether we acknowledge it or not. As Paul said: "*We can do nothing against the truth, only for it*" (2 Cor 13:8)

... Faith and Decision ...

So does it matter what we believe?

Absolutely!

Faith releases the benefit of the truth. (Heb 4:2). It is possible to continue living in ignorance and miss out on the enjoyment of what God has done for us. It is possible to continue living by our own strength and effort, ignoring the place of rest He prepared. This is why He still renews the promise daily saying: "*Today if you hear my voice, do not harden your hearts.*"

The more important question is how this faith is awakened and how man should be brought to this place of decision.

Eph 1:13 calls this message the "*word of truth, the gospel of your salvation*". This gospel is first and foremost a declaration of the truth as God knows it. It is the declaration of His persuasion. In it you are confronted with the reality of your salvation in Christ Jesus.

Rom 1:17 shows that in the gospel "*the righteousness of God is revealed from faith to faith*". It is from God's faith to our faith. Listen to how the Mirror translation says it: "*The secret of the Gospel is this: God did it right in Christ; the righteousness of God means that what happened in Christ, happened to us. His faith ignites ours. (From faith to faith) He is convinced about mankind and now persuades us to believe what He knows to be true about us. The prophets wrote in advance about this life of righteousness which would be based on faith and not on personal performance.*"

His faith ignites our faith! This is why Paul could say: "*The life I now live in the body, I live by the faith of the Son of God*" (Gal 2:20) Faith is not something we generate ourselves. The faith of God is contained within the declaration of the gospel - we can receive it or reject it, but we can never invalidate it or replace it with our own persuasions.

When man is presented with the reality of what God has done for and with man in Christ Jesus, it does not remove the need for faith, but greatly intensifies it. When we see the reality of God's opinion of us and how that contrasts with the reality of our experience, it creates a confrontation: do we want to live in God's reality or continue in the chaos and deception of our own opinions.

We also know that when anyone hears the word, he sees the face of his birth.[3] Once we've seen the truth about ourselves, we cannot reject it without rejecting our own existence.

It has to be emphasised that even this decision is not a mechanical formula that can be enforced on a person. This decision is based on the fact that God has made a decision

3 James 1:23

for us. He chose us and demonstrated His choice in Christ beyond doubt. His decision is to be one with you, to be reconciled to you, to make you His companion.

It was His choice to destroy our debt and guilt. It was His decision to unite us in His death and to present us blameless and innocent in His resurrection. It was His determined will to raise us up together with Him and seat us together with Him in heavenly places. How can we do anything but make a decision for Him, when we realise His decision for us!

God's election was demonstrated in the decisive action He took in Christ Jesus. His decision was to give Himself to us, to lavish His love upon humanity. In becoming man, He made known that His will and purpose is to be united with man. It is on the basis of this decision that we are enabled to make a decision for Him.

So what happens when a person receives Christ?

Receiving Christ is based on the truth that He already 'received', embraced and reconciled you! The scriptures reveal that grace and salvation were given to us before time began! (2 Tim 1:9). You were included in the life, death and resurrection of Christ - again, all of this happened before your birth. So in a sense, nothing changed - we simply wake up to God's reality.

Then again, everything changes for our eyes are opened for the first time when we meet Christ. The illusions and oppression of darkness lose their hold. God's reality has opportunity to find expression in your life! You start to know yourself as you have always been known. As a seed that germinates and produces after its own kind, the DNA of God is released to produce the God-kind of life He always knew was yours.

The gifts He so lavishly gave can now be adored, enjoyed and used for the first time. Eternal truth starts displacing temporal illusions. Life, original life, breaks through the hardened soil of self imposed ideas and opinions. This life is spontaneous, fresh, new, yet it is original, the life God designed and preserved for you even before your conception.

Meditation:

We can do nothing against the truth, only for it.

2 Cor 13:8

... looking unto Jesus, the author and finisher of faith.

Heb 12:2

Affirmation:

My faith is not blind ... it sees a greater reality than the physical. My faith did not originate in myself - Jesus is both the origin and the conclusion of faith. He persuades me of truth.

Discussion:

- Discuss the fact that truth remained true even before we believed it.
- Discuss the concept of 'from faith to faith' (Rom 1:17)

Assignment:

Write a short essay explaining how faith releases the benefit of the truth, using the example in Hebrews 4:1-10

Week 24
Incarnation Continues

"I continually thank my God for you because of the grace of God which is given you in Christ Jesus, that you are enriched by Him in every possible way, in all the fullness of what can be known and understood and being able to express it fully. Just as the evidence of Christ was confirmed within you - you have within yourselves the proof that He is! You don't lack anything - you are fully qualified. You have every reason to expect the Lord Jesus Christ to be made visible through you. Who also confirms your blamelessness to the uttermost degree in the day of our Lord Jesus Christ."
(1 Cor 1:4-8 WMF Translation)

Verse 5: ... in all utterance (logos) and all knowledge (gnosis).
The same *logos* that John wrote of - the *logos* that was in the beginning with God, and was God, the *logos* that became flesh in the person of Christ Jesus - this is the same *logos* with which we have been enriched. He has enriched us with all of Himself! Not just a portion or a fragment, but everything He is has been deposited in you. The same *logos* that became flesh in Christ, now becomes flesh in you! Col 2:3 speaks about all the treasures of wisdom and knowledge that are hidden in Him. If you have Him - you have all the

treasures of wisdom and knowledge!

This enrichment, this immeasurable deposit is not meant to remain quiet, unseen and undisturbed deep within you. We have every reason to expect Christ to express himself through us - an expression as full and accurate as the logos that was deposited in us. He anticipates that His DNA, from which you were born, will produce His God-kind of life in and through you. God sees no reason to expect any lesser manifestation of His life in you than in Jesus. You don't lack anything - you are fully qualified. You have every reason to expect the Lord Jesus Christ to be made visible through you.

The opening statement of the book of Acts is so enlightening. Luke writes "*about all that Jesus began to do and teach*". Jesus began something that now continues in us! In Acts 3 we read the story of Peter and John meeting a lame man on their way to the temple. This happened shortly after the ascension of Christ, so one could imagine Peter saying: "*I'm sorry, you've just missed Him. If only Jesus was still with us, we might have been able to offer you something*". Neither does Peter give the very spiritual advice that we have so often heard: "*Don't look at us - look at Jesus*"! No! Peter says: "*Look at us*" and then proceeds to heal this man!

Peter and John understood that what Jesus began, did not

end at His ascension. They understood that the same Logos, the same person that was manifested in Christ Jesus, was now at home in them. They understood that the incarnation continues; that God has united Himself with man, that His thoughts and person continues to find expression in those who accept the union He brought about in Christ.

Meditation:

You don't lack anything - you are fully qualified. You have every reason to expect the Lord Jesus Christ to be made visible through you.

1 Cor 1:7

Affirmation:

God's inspired thought ... His logic ... Logos ... found a home in me! Through me God is able to give expression to His thought - I am His poem.

Discussion:

- Discuss the significance of John 1:1 in relation to 1 Cor 1:5. The same Logos that became flesh in Christ Jesus, is in you!

Assignment:

Write a short essay celebrating the fact that the same Word that became flesh in Christ, has been invested in you.

Week 25
Discover Great Treasure

Paul spoke about treasure in earthen vessels.[1] In another letter He wrote about the "*the riches of His glorious inheritance in the saints*"[2]

Jesus spoke about this same treasure when He said: "*the kingdom of heaven is like treasure hidden in a field, which a man found and hid; and for joy over it he goes and sells all that he has and buys that field*". (Matthew 13:44)

God has invested everything He has, everything He is, in mankind. His treasure, His inheritance is located nowhere else but in mankind. The image and likeness of our Creator is what gives every man value. Proverbs speaks about the wisdom of God that was in the beginning. The same wisdom that John wrote about when he said the Word became flesh in the person of Christ. This is what proverbs says about this Wisdom: "*Then I was beside Him as a master craftsman; And I was daily His delight, Rejoicing always before Him, Rejoicing in His inhabited world, And my delight was in the sons of men.*" (Pr 8:30,31)

God's joy and delight has always been in the children of

1 2 Cor 4:7
2 Eph 1:18

men! If God's inheritance is in man, if He saw a treasure within humanity for which He paid the highest price, then we can find no greater value, no greater treasure than where He finds it. The greatest joy, delight and treasure, lies hidden in the next person you see!

It is this knowledge that inspired Paul to write that when it pleased God to reveal His Son in him, his immediate urgency was to proclaim Him (Christ) in the nations.[3] "*This mystery has been kept in the dark for a long time, but now it's out in the open. God wanted everyone, not just Jews, to know this rich and glorious secret inside and out, regardless of their background, regardless of their religious standing. The mystery in a nutshell is just this: Christ is in you, so therefore you can look forward to sharing in God's glory. It's that simple.*" (Col 1:26,27)

Recognising Christ, God's original design and blueprint of mankind, God's image and likeness in flesh form, is what drove Paul beyond the point of duty, to instruct every man about their perfection in Christ Jesus.

I love the way the Mirror Translation says this:
"*This mystery was concealed for ages and generations but is now fully realised in our restored innocence before Him. (God knows the mineral wealth that He deposited in the earth on man's behalf) in the same way He now eagerly*

3 Gal 1:16

anticipates the unveiling of the riches of the ultimate treasure in all the nations; which is Christ in you! The revelation of His indwelling fulfills His dream for you. This is the essence and focus of our message; we awaken every man's mind instructing every individual, bringing them into full enlightenment in order that we may exhibit the whole of mankind as perfect (without shortcoming and fully efficient) in Christ. To accomplish this, I am laboring beyond the point of exhaustion striving with intense resolve with all the energy that He mightily inspires within me." (Col 1:26-29)

I think Paul's whole motivation is summed up in Eph 3:9: "*to make all men see what is the fellowship of the mystery, which from the beginning of the ages has been hidden in God who created all things through Jesus Christ*". What he saw inspired him to make all men see, to go to any extent to help others see Christ in themselves, and themselves in Christ.

... *Eternal inheritance* ...

Our inheritance is so much more than a few perks we get for serving God! Our inheritance is exactly the same as God's inheritance: the treasure within man. I want to encourage you to discover this treasure in the people around you and in people far away. Don't limit your life to your job description; don't limit your life to some religious concept of special gifts and callings.

Part of the joy of finding great treasure is the pursuit, the journey, the adventure of searching for it beyond your familiar comfort zone.

"*Ask of Me, and I will give You the nations as Your inheritance, and the uttermost parts of the earth as Your possession.*" (Ps 2:8).

God has hidden treasure for each of us, in all the nations. He sees the impact of your life, uncontrollably expanding beyond your locality. Nothing but the uttermost parts of the earth is your inheritance! On one occasion Mother Teresa was asked why she chose to serve the poorest of the poor and part of her reply was: "*to discover Christ in the most distressing disguise!*"

Meditation:

Ask of Me, and I will give You the nations as Your inheritance, and the uttermost parts of the earth as Your possession."
Ps 2:8

Affirmation:

I carry the light of the revelation of Christ - the treasure that belongs to every man. To know Him and to make Him known inspires my life. God challenges me to ask Him for the nations ... Give me the nations Lord!

Discussion:

- What is your inheritance?
- What is the greatest treasure?

Assignment:

Write an imaginary story in which a whole city turns to God because of your testimony in it. There are some examples in the book of Acts in which entire cities and regions were turned upside down because of the testimony of believers.

The online 'Word Made Flesh' course includes the following:

- A hard-copy of the course (this book)
- Access to all the modules online.
- Audio downloads of the lessons.
- Access to an online class, consisting of other students.
- Assignments are done as discussion topics, allowing for interaction with other students.
- The discussions within a class are private, meaning that it is only visible to those registered for the course. Individuals are obviously free to republish content with the permission of the authors of that content.
- The weekly schedule and discussions contributes to a focussed experience.

The online course is available here:

ginomai.org

www.ingramcontent.com/pod-product-compliance
Lightning Source LLC
Chambersburg PA
CBHW070446090426
42735CB00012B/2470
9780956334640

WORD MADE FLESH

The ultimate destiny of God's Word was never a book, but His image and likeness displayed in human life!

This study guide to the written Word, is designed for this very purpose, to inspire and ignite an understanding that will find expression through our lives - the Word made flesh.

BY
ANDRE RABE

ISBN: 978-0-9563346-4-0

Published by Andre Rabe Publishing.

Contents